Kim Schaefer

BRIGHT&BOLD *COZY*
MODERN
Quilts

20 Projects · Easy Piecing · Stash Busting

C&T PUBLISHING

Text copyright © 2012 by Kim Schaefer

Photography and Artwork copyright © 2012
by C&T Publishing, Inc.

Publisher: Amy Marson

Creative Director: Gailen Runge

Art Director / Cover Designer: Kristy Zacharias

Editors: Lynn Koolish

Technical Editors: Helen Frost and Sadhana Wray

Book Designer: Kerry Graham

Production Coordinator: Jessica Jenkins

Production Editor: Alice Mace Nakanishi

Illustrator: Wendy Mathson

Photography by Christina Carty-Francis
and Diane Pedersen of C&T Publishing, Inc.,
unless otherwise noted

Published by C&T Publishing, Inc.,
P.O. Box 1456, Lafayette, CA 94549

Library of Congress Cataloging-in-Publication Data

Schaefer, Kim, 1960-

Bright & Bold Cozy Modern Quilts : 20 Projects - Easy
Piecing - Stash Busting / Kim Schaefer.

pages cm

ISBN 978-1-60705-441-2 (soft cover)

1. Patchwork--Patterns. 2. Machine quilting--Patterns.
3. Household linens. I. Title.

TT835.S28273 2012

746.46--dc23

2011049509

Printed in China

10 9 8 7 6 5 4 3 2 1

ACKNOWLEDGMENTS

My sincere thanks to the talented team of people at C&T Publishing for their professionalism and dedication to publishing the best books possible.

SPECIAL THANKS TO:

Lynn Koolish—it has been a pleasure to work with you again.

Helen Frost, my technical editor—thank you again for your technical editing expertise. My readers and I are lucky to have you checking and double-checking the patterns.

Wendy Mathson for the beautiful illustrations.

Diane Minkley of Patched Works, Inc. For years, Diane has been finishing my quilts so beautifully. I appreciate it more than I can say.

Finally, thank you to **my family** for their continued interest and support in all that I do.

CONTENTS

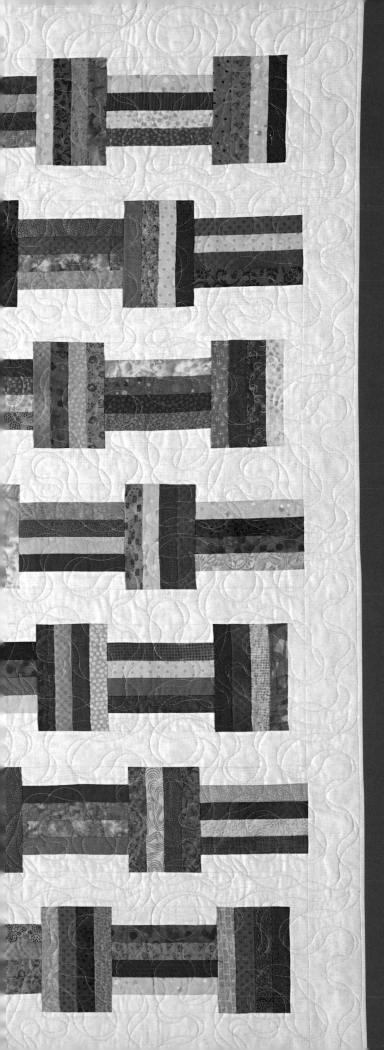

INTRODUCTION

In this follow-up to *Cozy Modern Quilts*, I have again tried to provide a collection of simply constructed, innovative designs for you to enjoy. All the projects are made from two simple shapes—the square and the rectangle. Many of the quilts are scrappy and offer a great opportunity to utilize your stash.

I have used many different fabrics in these projects, and as always, I encourage you to embrace your own personal style, whether it be traditional or contemporary. Color and fabric choices can dramatically affect a quilt's overall look. Through these choices, you will be able to create something that reflects who you are. The designs are versatile, and the patterns easily adapt to your style preference.

I have enjoyed designing this collection of projects. I hope this book will be a continued source of creativity and inspiration to you and that you will make some beautiful new quilts for friends and family to enjoy.

GENERAL INSTRUCTIONS

rotary cutting

I recommend that you cut all the fabrics used in the pieced blocks, borders, and bindings with a rotary cutter, an acrylic ruler, and a cutting mat. Trim the blocks and borders with these tools as well.

piecing

All piecing measurements include ¼" seam allowances. If you sew an accurate ¼" seam, you will succeed! My biggest and best quiltmaking tip is to learn to sew an accurate ¼" seam.

pressing

Press seams to one side, preferably toward the darker fabric. Press flat and avoid sliding the iron over the pieces, which can distort and stretch them. When you join two seamed sections, press the seams in opposite directions, so you can nest the seams and reduce bulk.

putting it all together

When all the blocks are completed for a project, lay them out on the floor or, if you are lucky enough to have one, a design wall. Arrange and rearrange the blocks until you are happy with the overall look. Each project has specific directions as well as diagrams and photos for assembly.

borders and lattice pieces

If the quilt borders or lattice pieces need to be longer than 40", join crosswise strips of fabric at a 45° angle as necessary and cut the strips to the desired length. All borders in the book are straight cut—none have mitered corners.

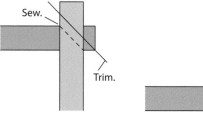

Join borders with 45° angle.

layering the quilt

Cut the batting and backing pieces 4"–5" larger than the quilt top. Place the pressed backing on the bottom with the right side down. Place the batting over the backing, and then place the quilt top on top, right side up. Make sure all the layers are flat and smooth and the quilt top is centered over the batting and backing. Pin or baste the quilt.

Since I prefer not to piece the backing for the runners, the fabric amounts allow for the length of the runner. Backings for quilts are pieced lengthwise unless otherwise noted. I use leftover fabric for bindings or add it to my stash.

> ### note
> If you are going to have your quilt quilted by a longarm quilter, contact the quilter for specific batting and backing requirements, as their information may differ from the instructions provided here.

quilting

Quilting is a personal choice, and you may prefer hand or machine quilting. My favorite method is to send the quilt top to a longarm quilter, as this method keeps my number of unfinished tops low and the number of finished quilts high.

color and fabric choices

I used 100% cotton fabrics in all the projects in this book. I find they are easy to work with and readily available at local quilt shops.

I have used both traditional and contemporary color choices, as well as a variety of fabrics, including batiks, solids, woven stripes, tone-on-tone prints, and some larger-scale contemporary prints. I have a very relaxed approach to color and tend to make my quilts very scrappy. The overall feel of a quilt can be changed dramatically by color and fabric choice, especially in pieced quilts.

Thankfully everyone has different tastes and preferences when it comes to color. Whether you prefer traditional, contemporary, or something in between, any of the designs can be adapted to your liking.

make the quilt your own

If you want to change the size of a quilt, simply add or subtract blocks or change the width of the borders. Many times, eliminating a border will give the quilt a more modern, contemporary look.

yardage and fabric requirements

I have given yardage and fabric requirements for each project, with many projects calling for a total amount of assorted fabrics that can be used as a base for your quilt. The yardage amounts may vary depending on several factors: the size of the quilt, the number of fabrics used, and the number of pieces you cut from each fabric. The fabric amounts are based on 42"-wide fabric.

The amounts given for binding allow for 2"-wide strips cut on the straight of grain. I usually use the same fabric for backing and binding, as this is a good way to use leftover backing fabric.

PROJECTS

This section contains a variety of projects, including lap quilts perfect for cuddling under as well as wall quilts and runners to decorate your home.

finishing

1. Layer the quilt top with batting and backing. Baste or pin.

2. Quilt as desired and bind.

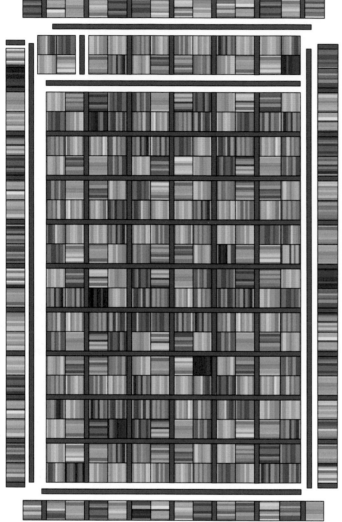

Putting It All Together

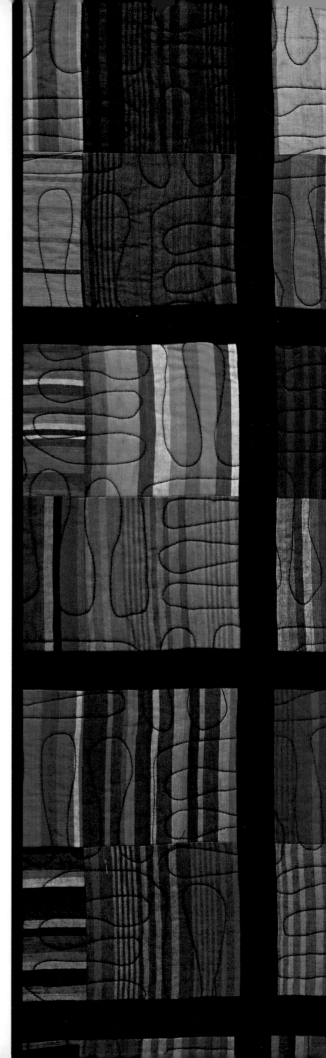

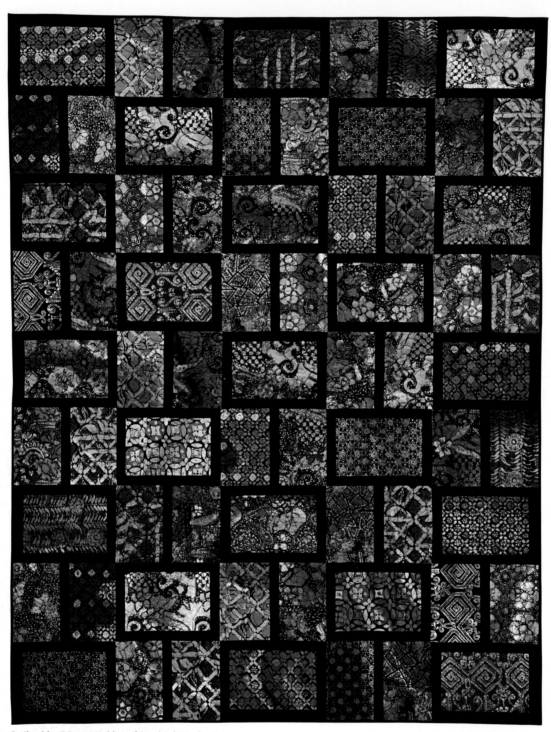

Quilted by Diane Minkley of Patched Works, Inc.

finished block size: 11″ × 8″ | finished lap quilt: 55½″ × 72½″

odessa lap quilt

This quilt is a great showcase for some of your favorite fabrics. The quilt is constructed using two simple blocks. I used hand-dyed batiks, but the simple design would also be perfect for solid fabrics or some of today's large-scale prints.

materials

- 3 yards total assorted batiks for pieced blocks

- 1½ yards black for pieced blocks

- 4 yards for backing (pieced crosswise) and binding

- 59″ × 76″ batting

cutting

Cut from assorted batiks:

- 23 rectangles 9½″ × 6½″ for pieced blocks

- 44 rectangles 5½″ × 8½″ for pieced blocks

Cut from black:

- 46 rectangles 1½″ × 6½″ for pieced blocks

- 46 rectangles 1½″ × 11½″ for pieced blocks

- 22 rectangles 1½″ × 8½″ for pieced blocks

piecing

BLOCK A

Piece Block A as shown. Press. Make 23 blocks.

Block A: Step 1

Step 2—Make 23.

BLOCK B

Piece Block B as shown. Press. Make 22 blocks.

Block B—Make 22.

putting it all together

1. Arrange and sew together the blocks in 9 rows of 5 blocks each. Refer to Putting It All Together (at right) as needed. Press.

2. Sew together the rows to form the quilt top. Press.

finishing

1. Layer the quilt with batting and backing. Baste or pin.

2. Quilt as desired and bind.

Putting It All Together

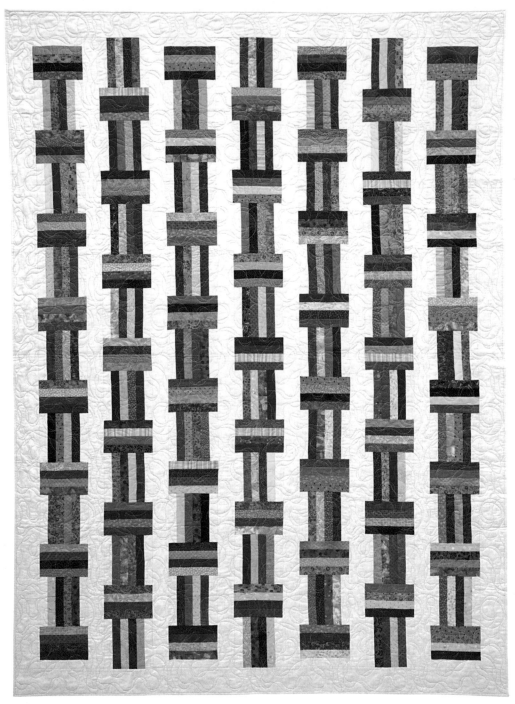

Quilted by Diane Minkley of Patched Works, Inc.

finished block sizes: BLOCK A 6″ × 6″   BLOCK B 6″ × 4″   BLOCK C 6″ × 5″ | finished lap quilt: 60½″ × 82½″

interweave lap quilt

A collection of bright pinks, yellows, and oranges surrounded by
a light lattice and border gives this quilt a fresh, cheerful look.

materials

- 3½ yards total assorted pinks, yellows, and oranges for pieced blocks

- 2¾ yards light for pieced blocks, lattice, and border

- 5 yards for backing and binding

- 65" × 87" batting

cutting

Cut a total of 420 rectangles 1½" × 6½" from assorted pinks, yellows, and oranges for pieced blocks.

Cut from light fabric:

- 112 rectangles 1½" × 6½" for pieced blocks

- 6 strips 2½" × 76½" for lattice

- 2 strips 3½" × 76½" for side borders

- 2 strips 3½" × 60½" for top and bottom borders

piecing

1. Piece Block A as shown. Press. Make 52 blocks.

Block A—Make 52.

2. Piece Block B as shown. Press. Make 45 blocks.

Block B—Make 45.

3. Piece Block C as shown. Press. Make 8 blocks.

Block C—Make 8.

putting it all together

QUILT CENTER

1. Arrange and sew together the blocks in 7 vertical rows of 15 blocks each. Refer to Putting It All Together (at right) as needed. Press.

2. Sew the lattice pieces between the rows to form the quilt top. Press.

BORDER

1. Sew the 2 side borders to the quilt top. Press toward the borders.

2. Sew the top and bottom borders to the quilt top. Press toward the borders.

finishing

1. Layer the quilt with batting and backing. Baste or pin.

2. Quilt as desired and bind.

Putting It All Together

Quilted by Diane Minkley of Patched Works, Inc.

finished block size: 10″ × 10″ | finished lap quilt: 65½″ × 85½″

maze madness lap quilt

The body of this quilt reminds me of the mazes I used to do as a child. Done in solid fabrics and framed by a chunky pieced border, this would make a great gift for a special child.

materials

- 2 yards light green for pieced blocks
- 4 yards total assorted brights for pieced blocks and pieced borders
- ¾ yard medium green for inner border
- 5¼ yards for backing and binding
- 70″ × 90″ batting

cutting

Cut from light green for Block A:

- 18 rectangles 1½″ × 2½″
- 36 rectangles 1½″ × 3½″
- 36 rectangles 1½″ × 5½″
- 18 rectangles 1½″ × 7½″
- 36 rectangles 1½″ × 8½″

Cut from each of 18 assorted brights for Block A:

- 2 rectangles 1½″ × 2½″
- 1 rectangle 1½″ × 3½″
- 2 rectangles 1½″ × 5½″
- 2 rectangles 1½″ × 7½″
- 1 rectangle 1½″ × 8½″
- 2 rectangles 1½″ × 10½″

Cut from light green for Block B:

- 17 rectangles 1½″ × 2½″
- 34 rectangles 1½″ × 3½″
- 17 rectangles 1½″ × 5½″
- 34 rectangles 1½″ × 6½″
- 34 rectangles 1½″ × 8½″
- 34 rectangles 1½″ × 10½″

Cut from each of 17 assorted brights for Block B:

- 2 rectangles 1½″ × 2½″
- 1 rectangle 1½″ × 3½″
- 2 rectangles 1½″ × 5½″
- 2 rectangles 1½″ × 7½″
- 1 rectangle 1½″ × 8½″

Cut from medium green for inner border:

- 2 strips 3″ × 70½″ for side borders
- 2 strips 3″ × 55½″ for top and bottom borders

Cut 56 squares 5½″ × 5½″ from assorted brights for outer pieced border.

piecing

BLOCK A

Piece Block A as shown. Press. Make 18 blocks.

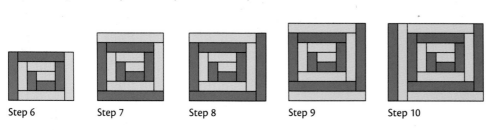

Step 1   Step 2   Step 3   Step 4   Step 5

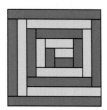

Step 6   Step 7   Step 8   Step 9   Step 10

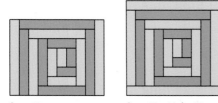

Step 11—Make 18.

BLOCK B

Piece Block B as shown. Press. Make 17 blocks.

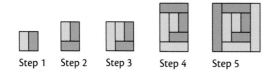

Step 1   Step 2   Step 3   Step 4   Step 5

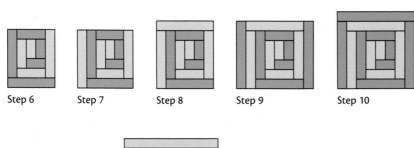

Step 6   Step 7   Step 8   Step 9   Step 10

Step 11   Step 12—Make 17.

putting it all together

QUILT CENTER

1. Arrange and sew together the blocks in 7 rows of 5 blocks each. Refer to Putting It All Together (at right) as needed. Press.

2. Sew together the rows to form the quilt top. Press.

INNER BORDER

1. Sew the 2 side borders to the quilt top. Press toward the borders.

2. Sew the top and bottom borders to the quilt top. Press toward the borders.

OUTER PIECED BORDER

1. Arrange and sew together 2 rows of 15 squares each for the 2 side borders. Press.

2. Sew the 2 side borders to the quilt top. Press toward the inner borders.

3. Arrange and sew together 2 rows of 13 squares each for the top and bottom borders. Press.

4. Sew the top and bottom borders to the quilt top. Press toward the inner borders.

finishing

1. Layer the quilt top with batting and backing. Baste or pin.

2. Quilt as desired and bind.

Putting It All Together

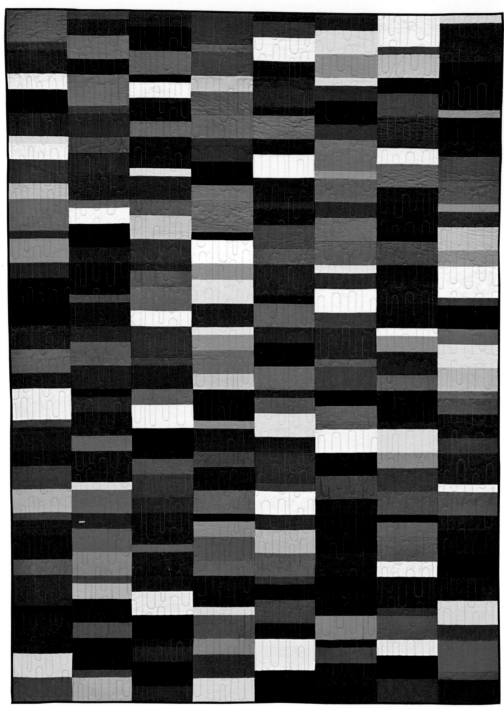

Quilted by Diane Minkley of Patched Works, Inc.

finished block size: 8″ × 8″ | finished lap quilt: 64½″ × 88½″

baxter lap quilt

The solid fabrics used in this quilt give it a modern, graphic look. The quilt was cut and pieced in one day!
It is a great project for beginners and gives more experienced quilters a chance to explore color.

materials

- ¼ yard each of 25 different solids for pieced blocks

- 5½ yards for backing and binding

- 69″ × 93″ batting

cutting

Cut from assorted solids for pieced blocks:

- 59 rectangles 1½″ × 8½″

- 87 rectangles 2½″ × 8½″

- 117 rectangles 3½″ × 8½″

- 30 rectangles 4½″ × 8½″

piecing

1. For each Block A, arrange and sew together a 4½″ × 8½″ rectangle, a 1½″ × 8½″ rectangle, and a 3½″ × 8½″ rectangle. Press. Make 30 blocks.

Block A—Make 30.

2. For each Block B, arrange and sew together a 2½″ × 8½″ rectangle and 2 rectangles 3½″ × 8½″. Press. Make 29 blocks.

Block B—Make 29.

3. For each Block C, arrange and sew together a 1½″ × 8½″ rectangle, 2 rectangles 2½″ × 8½″, and a 3½″ × 8½″ rectangle. Press. Make 29 blocks.

Block C—Make 29.

putting it all together

1. Arrange and sew together the blocks in 8 vertical rows of 11 blocks each. Refer to Putting It All Together (below) as needed. Press.

2. Sew together the rows to form the quilt top. Press.

finishing

1. Layer the quilt top with batting and backing. Baste or pin.

2. Quilt as desired and bind.

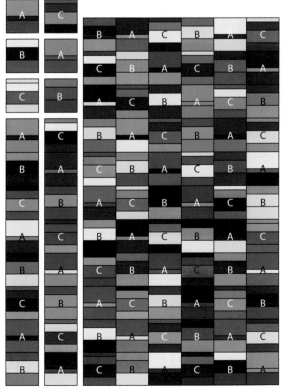

Putting It All Together

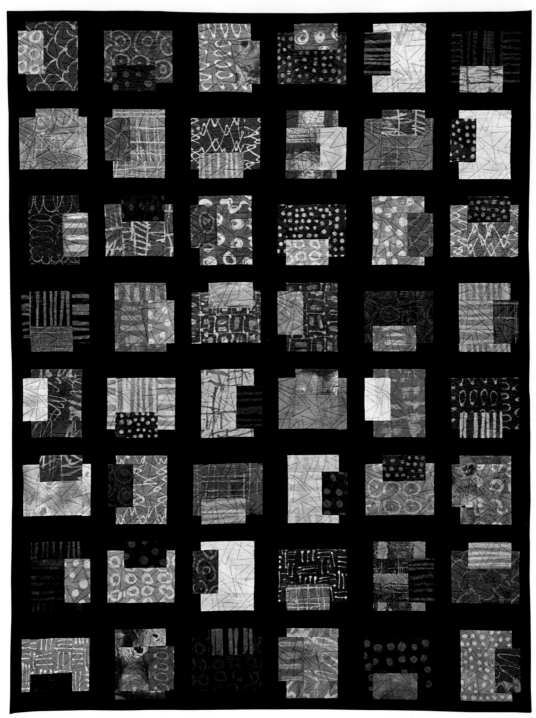

Quilted by Diane Minkley of Patched Works, Inc.

finished block size: 10″ × 10″ | finished lap quilt: 60½″ × 80½″

around the square lap quilt

I love combining bright fabrics with earthy tones. These fabrics have a
hand-dyed look but are actually commercial prints. The quilt is made with
a single block of overlapping rectangles, which gives it a modern look.

materials

- 3 yards black for pieced blocks
- 2¾ yards total assorted brights for pieced blocks
- 5 yards for backing and binding
- 65" × 85" batting

cutting

Cut from black for pieced blocks:

- 96 rectangles 1½" × 10½"
- 96 squares 2½" × 2½"
- 96 rectangles 1½" × 2½"
- 48 rectangles 1½" × 5½"
- 48 rectangles 2½" × 5½"

Cut from assorted brights for pieced blocks:

- 48 rectangles 1½" × 6½"
- 48 rectangles 4½" × 5½"
- 48 rectangles 2½" × 6½"

Cut from contrasting assorted brights for pieced blocks:

- 48 rectangles 3½" × 5½"

piecing

Piece the blocks as shown. Press. Make 48 blocks.

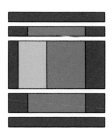

Piece blocks.

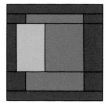

Make 48.

putting it all together

1. Arrange and sew together the blocks in 8 rows of 6 blocks each. Refer to Putting It All Together (at right) as needed. Press.

2. Sew together the rows to form the quilt top. Press.

finishing

1. Layer the quilt top with batting and backing. Baste or pin.

2. Quilt as desired and bind.

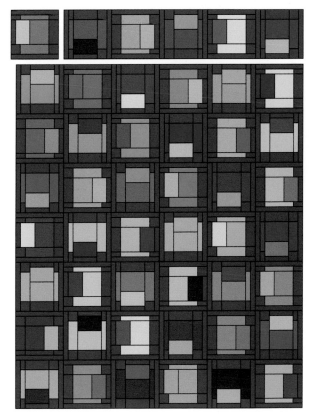

Putting It All Together

Quilted by Diane Minkley of Patched Works, Inc.

finished block size: 10″ × 10″ | finished lap quilt: 50½″ × 70½″

pause lap quilt

This quilt's simple design makes it a fast and easy project. Tone-on-tone
fabrics in blues and greens give it a modern feeling.

materials

- 2¼ yards total assorted blues for pieced blocks
- 2¼ yards total assorted greens for pieced blocks
- 3¾ yards for backing (pieced crosswise) and binding
- 55″ × 75″ batting

cutting

Cut from assorted blues for pieced blocks:
- 88 rectangles 2½″ × 8½″
- 36 rectangles 1½″ × 10½″

Cut from assorted greens for pieced blocks:
- 87 rectangles 2½″ × 8½″
- 34 rectangles 1½″ × 10½″

piecing

BLOCK A

Piece Block A as shown. Press. Make 18 blocks.

Block A: Step 1

Step 2—Make 18.

BLOCK B

Piece Block B as shown. Press. Make 17 blocks.

Block B: Step 1

Step 2—Make 17.

putting it all together

1. Arrange and sew together the blocks in 7 rows of 5 blocks each. Refer to Putting It All Together (below) as needed. Press.

2. Sew together the rows to form the quilt top. Press.

finishing

1. Layer the quilt with batting and backing. Baste or pin.

2. Quilt as desired and bind.

Putting It All Together

Quilted by Diane Minkley of Patched Works, Inc.

finished lap quilt: 76½" × 88½"

zip strip lap quilt

Warm, cozy flannel was used in this easy-to-piece strip quilt.
The flannel makes it a perfect quilt for cuddling under.

materials

- 5¼ yards total assorted textured solids for quilt center and pieced border
- 1½ yards black for lattice and inner borders
- 6¼ yards for backing and binding
- 81" × 93" batting

cutting

Cut 269 rectangles 2½" × 10½" from assorted solids for quilt center and pieced borders. (Cut 10½" strips first, and then subcut 2½" × 10½" rectangles from the strips.)

Cut from black:

- 6 strips 3½" × 50½" for lattice and top and bottom inner borders
- 2 strips 3½" × 68½" for 2 side inner borders

piecing

Arrange and sew together the rectangles in 5 rows of 25 rectangles each. Refer to Putting It All Together (at right) as needed. Press.

putting it all together

QUILT CENTER

1. Sew the horizontal lattice pieces between the rows. Press.

2. Sew the top and bottom inner borders to the quilt top. Press toward the borders.

3. Sew the 2 side borders to the quilt top. Press toward the borders.

OUTER PIECED BORDER

1. Arrange and sew together 2 rows of 34 rectangles each for the 2 side borders. Press.

2. Sew the 2 side borders to the quilt top. Press toward the borders.

3. Arrange and sew together 2 rows of 38 rectangles each for the top and bottom borders. Press.

4. Sew the top and bottom borders to the quilt top. Press toward the borders.

finishing

1. Layer the quilt top with batting and backing. Baste or pin.

2. Quilt as desired and bind.

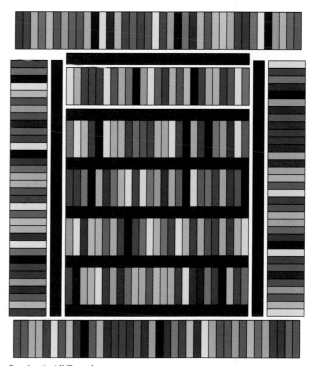

Putting It All Together

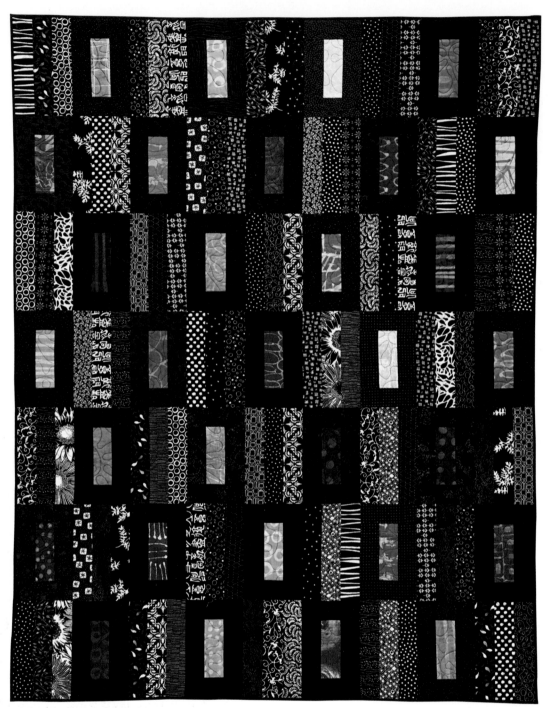

Quilted by Diane Minkley of Patched Works, Inc.

finished block size: 6″ × 10″ | finished wall quilt: 54½″ × 70½″

hoytyville wall quilt

Black-and-white prints are mixed with brightly colored fabrics
in this simple two-block quilt made from 2½″ strips.

materials

- 2 yards total assorted black-and-white prints for pieced blocks
- 1¾ yards total assorted black tone-on-tone prints for pieced blocks
- ½ yard total assorted brights for pieced blocks
- 3¾ yards for backing (pieced crosswise) and binding
- 59″ × 75″ batting

cutting

Cut 96 rectangles 2½″ × 10½″ from assorted black-and-white prints for pieced blocks.

Cut 124 rectangles 2½″ × 6½″ from black tone-on-tone prints for pieced blocks.

Cut 31 rectangles 2½″ × 6½″ from assorted brights for pieced blocks.

piecing

BLOCK A

Piece Block A as shown. Press. Make 32 blocks.

Block A—Make 32.

BLOCK B

Piece Block B as shown. Press. Make 31 blocks.

Block B: Step 1

Step 2—Make 31.

putting it all together

1. Arrange and sew together the blocks in 7 rows of 9 blocks each. Refer to Putting It All Together (below) as needed. Press.

2. Sew together the rows to form the quilt top. Press.

finishing

1. Layer the quilt top with batting and backing. Baste or pin.

2. Quilt as desired and bind.

Putting It All Together

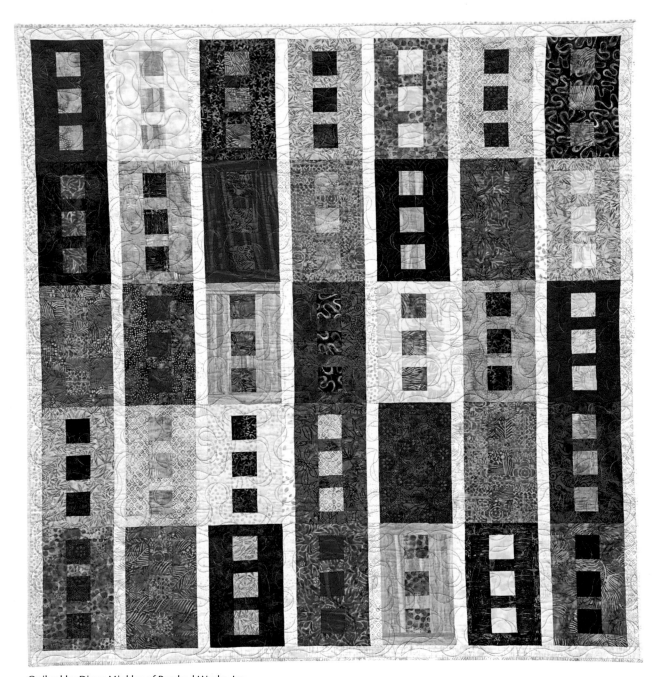

Quilted by Diane Minkley of Patched Works, Inc.

finished block size: 6" × 10" | finished wall quilt: 50½" × 52½"

city lights wall quilt

A light, vertical lattice separates brightly colored batiks in this easy-to-piece row quilt.
A monochromatic palette would work for this fun design as well.

materials

- 2¾ yards total assorted bright batiks for pieced blocks

- 1 yard total assorted light batiks for lattice and borders

- 3½ yards for backing and binding

- 55″ × 57″ batting

cutting

Cut from assorted bright batiks for pieced blocks (2 for each block):

- 70 rectangles 2½″ × 8½″

- 70 rectangles 1½″ × 6½″

- 70 rectangles 1½″ × 2½″

Cut 105 squares 2½″ × 2½″ from contrasting assorted bright batiks for pieced blocks (3 for each block).

Cut from assorted light batiks:

- 30 rectangles 1½″ × 10½″ for lattice

- 2 strips 1½″ × 50½″ for side borders

- 2 strips 1½″ × 50½″ for top and bottom borders

---

piecing

Piece the blocks as shown. Press. Make 35 blocks.

Step 1   Step 2

Step 3—Make 35.

putting it all together

QUILT CENTER

1. Arrange the blocks into 5 rows of 7 blocks each. Refer to Putting It All Together (at right) as needed. Press.

2. Sew the lattice pieces between the blocks. Press.

3. Sew together the rows. Press.

BORDER

1. Sew the 2 side borders to the quilt top. Press toward the borders.

2. Sew the top and bottom borders to the quilt top. Press toward the borders.

finishing

1. Layer the quilt top with batting and backing. Baste or pin.

2. Quilt as desired and bind.

Putting It All Together

Quilted by Diane Minkley of Patched Works, Inc.

finished block size: 10″ × 10″ | finished wall quilt: 56½″ × 56½″

kaleidoscope wall quilt

Large blocks cut into quarters and then pieced back together make this quilt look much more complicated than it really is. For best results, alternate warm and cool colors throughout the quilt.

materials

- 3¼ yards total assorted bright prints for pieced blocks
- 1 yard green for lattice and borders
- 3¾ yards for backing and binding
- 61″ × 61″ batting

cutting

Cut from assorted bright prints for pieced blocks:

- 25 squares 7″ × 7″
- 50 rectangles 2½″ × 7″
- 50 rectangles 2½″ × 11″

Cut from green:

- 20 rectangles 1½″ × 10½″ for vertical lattice
- 6 strips 1½″ × 54½″ for horizontal lattice and side borders
- 2 strips 1½″ × 56½″ for top and bottom borders

piecing

1. Piece the blocks as shown. Press. Make 25 blocks.

Step 1   Step 2—Make 25.

2. Cut the 25 pieced blocks into quarters, each measuring 5½″ × 5½″. Make 100 quarters.

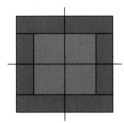

Cut blocks into quarters.

3. Arrange and sew the quarters into blocks. NOTE: I placed the pieces randomly and didn't worry whether the direction of the seams was consistent. Press. Make 25 blocks.

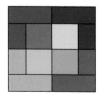

Sew quarters into blocks; make 25.

putting it all together

QUILT CENTER

1. Arrange the blocks into 5 rows of 5 blocks each.

2. Sew the vertical lattice pieces between the blocks. Refer to Putting It All Together (below) as needed. Press.

3. Sew the horizontal lattice pieces between the rows to form the quilt top. Press.

BORDER

1. Sew the 2 side borders to the quilt top. Press toward the borders.

2. Sew the top and bottom borders to the quilt top. Press toward the borders.

finishing

1. Layer the quilt top with batting and backing. Baste or pin.

2. Quilt as desired and bind.

Putting It All Together

Quilted by Diane Minkley of Patched Works, Inc.

finished block size: 11″ × 14″ | finished wall quilt: 59½″ × 60½″

ladora wall quilt

Concentric rectangles are the focal point of this quilt, which was made with brown and blue batiks with backgrounds of soft warm grays and off-whites. The quilt has a casual yet elegant feeling.

materials

- 1½ yards total assorted white batiks for pieced backgrounds
- 1¼ yards total assorted gray batiks for pieced background and pieced blocks
- 1¼ yards total assorted brown batiks for pieced blocks
- 1 yard total assorted blue batiks for pieced blocks
- 3¾ yards for backing and binding
- 64" × 65" batting

cutting

Cut from assorted white batiks for pieced backgrounds:
- 16 rectangles 4½" × 6½"
- 16 rectangles 3½" × 4½"
- 10 rectangles 3½" × 7½"
- 10 rectangles 3½" × 14½"

Cut from assorted gray batiks for pieced backgrounds:
- 23 rectangles 3½" × 6½"
- 8 squares 3½" × 3½"

Cut from assorted gray batiks for pieced blocks:
- 12 rectangles 1½" × 4½"
- 12 rectangles 1½" × 6½"
- 12 rectangles 1½" × 5½"

Cut from assorted brown batiks for pieced blocks:
- 12 rectangles 1½" × 4½"
- 12 rectangles 1½" × 3½"
- 12 rectangles 1½" × 5½"
- 12 rectangles 1½" × 6½"
- 12 rectangles 3½" × 8½"
- 12 rectangles 3½" × 11½"

Cut from assorted blue batiks for pieced blocks:
- 12 rectangles 1½" × 4½"
- 12 rectangles 1½" × 3½"
- 12 rectangles 3½" × 8½"
- 12 rectangles 3½" × 11½"

piecing

BLOCK A

Piece Block A as shown. Press. Make 6 blocks.

Step 1   Step 2   Step 3   Step 4   Step 5   Step 6—Make 6.

BLOCK B

Piece Block B as shown. Press. Make 6 blocks.

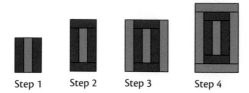

Step 1   Step 2   Step 3   Step 4

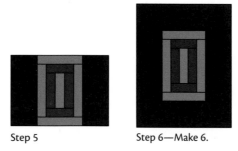

Step 5   Step 6—Make 6.

BACKGROUND

1. Piece the background sections as shown. Press.

Piece background sections; make 8.

Piece background sections; make 8.

2. Piece the vertical background sections as shown. Press.

Piece vertical background sections; make 5.

putting it all together

1. Arrange and sew together the blocks and background sections into 4 vertical rows. Refer to Putting It All Together (below) as needed. Press.

2. Sew the vertical background sections between the rows and on the sides to form the quilt top. Press.

finishing

1. Layer the quilt top with batting and backing. Baste or pin.

2. Quilt as desired and bind.

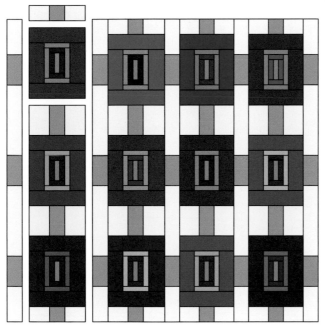

Putting It All Together

Quilted by Diane Minkley of Patched Works, Inc.

finished block size: 5″ × 10″ | finished wall quilt: 45½″ × 50½″

broken glass wall quilt

Two simple blocks are alternated to create a striking design in this fast and easy wall quilt.

materials

- 2 yards total assorted green and teal prints for pieced blocks

- ⅜ yard brown for pieced blocks

- 3¼ yards for backing and binding

- 50″ × 55″ batting

cutting

Cut from assorted greens and teals for pieced blocks:

- 46 rectangles 1½″ × 5½″

- 46 rectangles 2½″ × 8½″

Cut 22 rectangles 5½″ × 10½″ from assorted greens and teals for alternate blocks.

Cut 23 rectangles 1½″ × 8½″ from brown for pieced blocks.

piecing

Piece the blocks as shown. Press. Make 23 blocks.

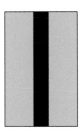

Step 1

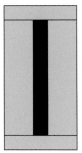

Step 2—Make 23.

putting it all together

1. Arrange and sew together the blocks in 5 rows of 9 blocks each. Refer to Putting It All Together (at right) as needed. Press.

2. Sew together the rows to form the quilt top. Press.

finishing

1. Layer the quilt top with batting and backing. Baste or pin.

2. Quilt as desired and bind.

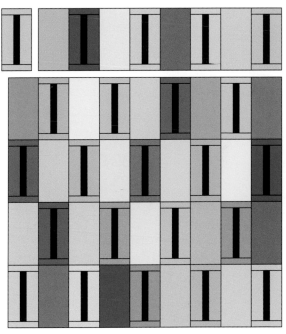

Putting It All Together

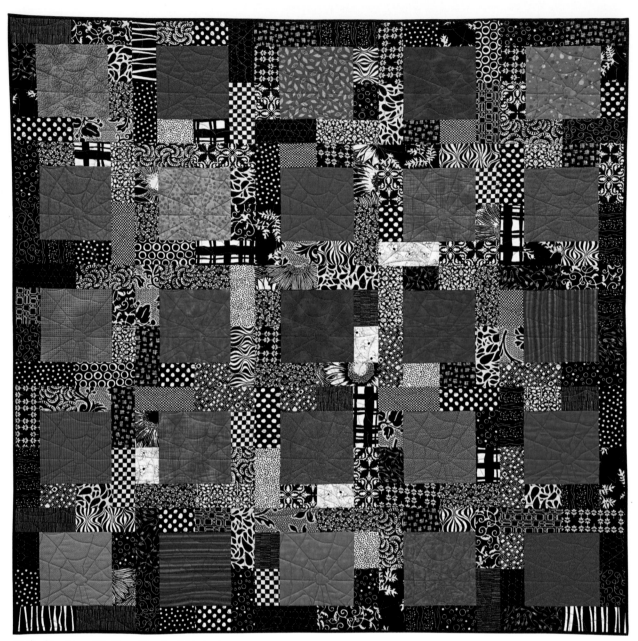

Quilted by Diane Minkley of Patched Works, Inc.

finished block size: 10″ × 10″ | finished wall quilt: 50½″ × 50½″

moxie wall quilt

Black-and-white prints are paired with bright oranges to create this stunningly graphic quilt. Not a fan of orange? Substitute red, lime green, teal, blue, or purple—you choose—to achieve the same graphic results.

materials

- 2 yards total assorted black-and-white prints for pieced blocks

- 1¼ yards total assorted oranges for pieced blocks

- 3¼ yards for backing and binding

- 55″ × 55″ batting

cutting

Cut from assorted black-and-white prints for pieced blocks:

- 100 rectangles 2½″ × 3½″

- 100 rectangles 2½″ × 5½″

Cut 25 squares 6½″ × 6½″ from assorted oranges for pieced blocks.

piecing

Piece the blocks as shown. Press. Make 25 blocks.

Step 1

Step 2

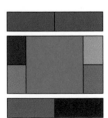

Step 3

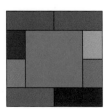

Step 4—Make 25.

putting it all together

1. Arrange and sew together the blocks in 5 rows of 5 blocks each. Refer to Putting It All Together (below) as needed. Press.

2. Sew together the rows to form the quilt top. Press.

finishing

1. Layer the quilt top with batting and backing. Baste or pin.

2. Quilt as desired and bind.

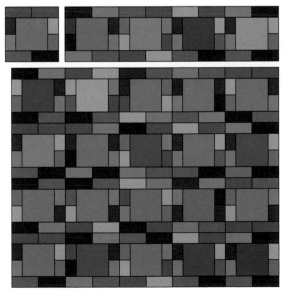

Putting It All Together

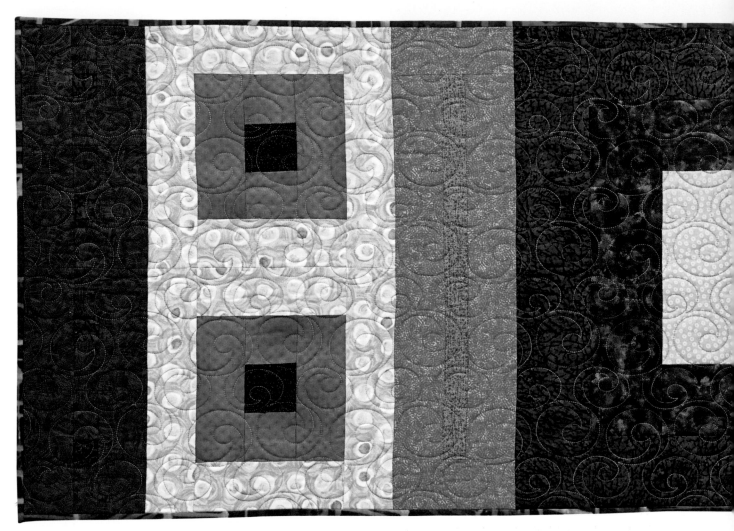

Quilted by Diane Minkley of Patched Works, Inc.

finished block sizes: BLOCK A 20″ × 20″ BLOCK B 20″ × 5″ BLOCK C 10″ × 10″ BLOCK D 5″ × 5″

finished runner: 20½″ × 60½″

playtime runner

Contrasting colors and simple pieced blocks are combined to create this whimsical runner.

materials

- 1¾ yards total assorted purples, greens, and teals for pieced blocks

- 1⅞ yards for backing and binding

- 25″ × 65″ batting

cutting

The pieces for each matching set of squares and rectangles are listed together.

BLOCK A (Make 1.)

Cut from assorted colors:

- 1 square 8½″ × 8½″

- 2 rectangles 3½″ × 8½″ and 2 rectangles 3½″ × 14½″

- 2 rectangles 3½″ × 14½″ and 2 rectangles 3½″ × 20½″

BLOCK B (Make 2.)

Cut from assorted colors:

- 2 rectangles 1½″ × 16½″

- 4 rectangles 2½″ × 16½″ and 4 rectangles 2½″ × 5½″

BLOCK C (Make 4.)

Cut from assorted colors:

- 4 squares 2½″ × 2½″

- 8 squares 2½″ × 2½″ and 8 rectangles 2½″ × 6½″

- 8 rectangles 2½″ × 6½″ and 8 rectangles 2½″ × 10½″

BLOCK D (Make 8.)

Cut from assorted colors:

- 8 squares 1½″ × 1½″

- 16 rectangles 2½″ × 5½″ and 16 rectangles 1½″ × 2½″

piecing

BLOCK A

Piece Block A as shown. Press.

Block A: Step 1

Step 2

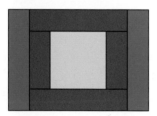

Step 3

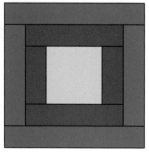

Step 4—Make 1.

BLOCK B

Piece Block B as shown. Press.

Block B: Step 1

Step 2—Make 2.

BLOCK C

Piece Block C as shown. Press.

Block C: Step 1

Step 2

Step 3

Step 4—Make 4.

BLOCK D

Piece Block D as shown. Press.

Block D: Step 1

Step 2—Make 8.

putting it all together

1. Arrange the blocks into sections as shown. Refer to Putting It All Together (below) as needed.

2. Sew together the sections to form the runner top. Press.

finishing

1. Layer the runner top with batting and backing. Baste or pin.

2. Quilt as desired and bind.

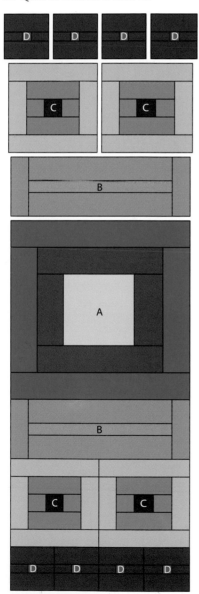

Putting It All Together

Quilted by Diane Minkley of Patched Works, Inc.

finished block size: 5" × 10" | finished runner: 15½" × 60½"

materials

- 1⅓ yards total assorted pink, orange, and red solids for pieced blocks

- 1⅞ yards for backing and binding

- 20" × 65" batting

cutting

Cut from assorted pink, orange, and red solids:

- 36 rectangles 2½" × 10½" (2 for each block)

- 72 squares 1½" × 1½" (4 for each block)

Cut from contrasting assorted pink, orange, and red solids:

- 54 rectangles 1½" × 2½" (3 for each block)

piecing

Piece the blocks as shown. Press. Make 18 blocks.

Step 1

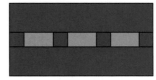

Step 2—Make 18.

making tracks runner

Fast and easy to piece, this contemporary design is perfect for today's modern quilter.

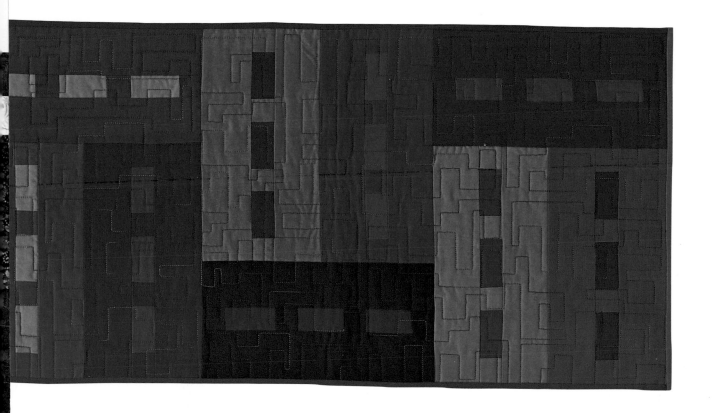

putting it all together

1. Arrange and sew together the blocks in 6 sections of 3 blocks each. Sew the sections into rows. Refer to Putting It All Together (at right) as needed. Press.

2. Sew together the rows. Press.

finishing

1. Layer the runner top with batting and backing. Baste or pin.

2. Quilt as desired and bind.

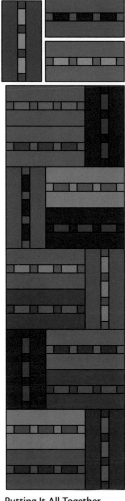

Putting It All Together

Quilted by Diane Minkley of Patched Works, Inc.

finished runner: 20½″ × 70½″

materials

- 1¼ yards total assorted green batiks

- 1 yard total assorted purple batiks

- 2¼ yards for backing and binding

- 25″ × 75″ batting

cutting

Cut from assorted green batiks:

- 2 rectangles 1″ × 14½″

- 1 rectangle 1½″ × 14½″

- 1 rectangle 2½″ × 14½″

- 2 rectangles 3″ × 14½″

- 2 rectangles 3½″ × 14½″

- 1 rectangle 5″ × 14½″

- 5 rectangles 5½″ × 14½″

- 6 rectangles 1″ × 3½″

- 6 rectangles 1½″ × 3½″

- 2 rectangles 2″ × 3½″

- 10 rectangles 2½″ × 3½″

- 2 rectangles 3″ × 3½″

- 2 squares 3½″ × 3½″

- 2 rectangles 4½″ × 3½″

Cut from assorted purple batiks:

- 3 rectangles 1″ × 14½″

- 3 rectangles 1½″ × 14½″

- 1 rectangle 2″ × 14½″

- 5 rectangles 2½″ × 14½″

- 1 rectangle 3″ × 14½″

- 1 rectangle 3½″ × 14½″

- 1 rectangle 4½″ × 14½″

- 4 rectangles 1″ × 3½″

- 2 rectangles 1½″ × 3½″

- 2 rectangles 2½″ × 3½″

- 4 rectangles 3″ × 3½″

- 4 squares 3½″ × 3½″

- 2 rectangles 5″ × 3½″

- 10 rectangles 5½″ × 3½″

geneva runner

Batiks in rich greens and purples are used to create this easy-to-piece runner.

putting it all together

1. Arrange and sew together the runner in horizontal sections, adding green rectangles to purple rectangles of the same width and vice versa. Arrange the sections as desired. Refer to Putting It All Together (at right) as needed. Press.

2. Sew together the horizontal sections to form the runner. Press.

finishing

1. Layer the runner top with batting and backing. Baste or pin.

2. Quilt as desired and bind.

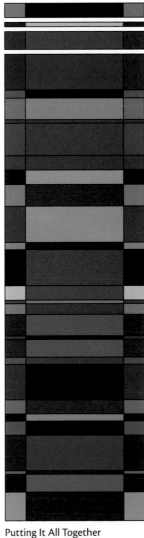

Putting It All Together

Quilted by Diane Minkley of Patched Works, Inc.
finished block size: 8″ × 8″ | finished runner: 24½″ × 56½″

materials

- 1¼ yards total assorted gray batiks for pieced blocks

- 1¼ yards total assorted purple batiks for pieced blocks

- 1¾ yards for backing and binding

- 29″ × 61″ batting

cutting

Cut from assorted gray batiks for pieced blocks:

- 44 squares 3½″ × 3½″

- 20 rectangles 1½″ × 6½″

- 20 rectangles 1½″ × 8½″

Cut from assorted purple batiks for pieced blocks:

- 40 squares 3½″ × 3½″

- 22 rectangles 1½″ × 6½″

- 22 rectangles 1½″ × 8½″

purple mist runner

Simple framed blocks made from 3″ squares are pieced together to create this runner with classic appeal.

putting it all together

1. Arrange and sew together the blocks in 7 rows of 3 blocks each. Refer to Putting It All Together (below) as needed. Press.

2. Sew together the rows to form the runner top. Press.

finishing

1. Layer the runner top with batting and backing. Baste or pin.

2. Quilt as desired and bind.

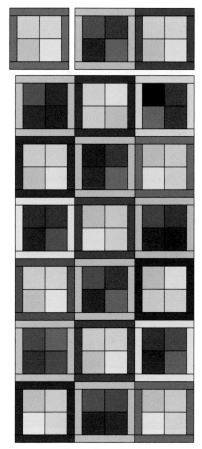

Putting It All Together

piecing

BLOCK A

Piece Block A as shown. Press. Make 11 blocks.

  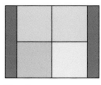

Block A: Step 1   Step 2   Step 3

Step 4—Make 11.

BLOCK B

Piece Block B as shown. Press. Make 10 blocks.

  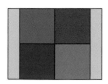

Block B: Step 1   Step 2   Step 3

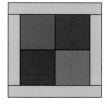

Step 4—Make 10.

Quilted by Diane Minkley of Patched Works, Inc.

finished block sizes:

BLOCK A 10″ × 10″   BLOCK B 10″ × 10″   BLOCK C 5″ × 5″   BLOCK D 5″ × 5″   BLOCK E 10″ × 10″

BLOCK F 10″ × 10″   BLOCK G 10″ × 10″   BLOCK H 10″ × 10″   BLOCK I 10″ × 10″

finished runner: 24½″ × 54½″

materials

- 1¾ yards total assorted prints for runner center and pieced border

- 1¾ yards for backing and binding

- 29″ × 59″ batting

cutting

The pieces for each set of rectangles are listed together.

BLOCK A (Make 2.)

Cut from assorted prints:

- 2 squares 2½″ × 2½″ for centers

- 4 rectangles 2½″ × 3½″ and 4 rectangles 3½″ × 8½″

- 2 rectangles 1½″ × 8½″ and 2 rectangles 1½″ × 10½″

soft walk runner

Soft, subtle fabrics are used to create this pieced block runner.
It's sure to add sophisticated elegance to any decor.

BLOCK G (Make 1.)

Cut from assorted prints:

- 1 square 6½" × 6½" for center

- 2 rectangles 1½" × 6½"
  and 2 rectangles 1½" × 8½"

- 2 rectangles 1½" × 8½" and
  2 rectangles 1½" × 10½"

BLOCK H (Make 1.)

Cut from assorted prints:

- 1 square 4½" × 4½" for center

- 2 rectangles 1½" × 4½"
  and 2 rectangles 1½" × 6½"

- 2 rectangles 2½" × 6½"
  and 2 rectangles 2½" × 10½"

BLOCK I (Make 1.)

Cut from assorted prints:

- 1 square 4½" × 4½" for center

- 2 rectangles 3½" × 4½"
  and 2 rectangles 3½" × 10½"

SIDE BORDERS (Make 2.)

Cut from assorted prints:

- 14 squares 2½" × 2½"

- 4 rectangles 2½" × 3½"

- 2 rectangles 2½" × 5½"

- 2 rectangles 2½" × 6½"

- 2 rectangles 2½" × 8½"

- 2 rectangles 2½" × 11½"

END BORDERS (Make 2.)

Cut from assorted prints:

- 4 squares 2½" × 2½"

- 2 rectangles 2½" × 3½"

- 2 rectangles 2½" × 4½"

- 2 rectangles 2½" × 6½"

- 2 rectangles 2½" × 7½"

BLOCK B (Make 1.)

Cut from assorted prints:

- 1 square 6½" × 6½" for center

- 2 rectangles 2½" × 6½"
  and 2 rectangles 2½" × 10½"

BLOCK C (Make 5.)

Cut from assorted prints
5 squares 5½" × 5½".

BLOCK D (Make 3.)

Cut from assorted prints:

- 3 squares 1½" × 1½" for centers

- 6 rectangles 1½" × 2½"
  and 6 rectangles 2½" × 5½"

BLOCK E (Make 1.)

Cut from assorted prints:

- 1 square 4½" × 4½" for center

- 2 rectangles 2½" × 4½"
  and 2 rectangles 2½" × 8½"

- 2 rectangles 1½" × 8½"
  and 2 rectangles 1½" × 10½"

BLOCK F (Make 1.)

Cut from assorted prints:

- 1 square 2½" × 2½" for center

- 2 rectangles 2½" × 4½"
  and 2 rectangles 4½" × 10½"

about the author

Kim Schaefer began sewing at an early age and was quilting seriously by the late 1980s. Her early quilting career included designing and producing small quilts for craft shows and shops across the country.

In 1986, Kim founded Little Quilt Company, a pattern company focused on designing a variety of small, fun-to-make projects.

In addition to designing quilt patterns, Kim is a best-selling author for C&T Publishing. Kim also designs fabric for Andover/Makower and works with Leo Licensing, which licenses her designs for nonfabric products.

Kim lives with her family in southeastern Wisconsin.

For more information on Little Quilt Company, please visit www.littlequiltcompany.com, which offers Kim's entire collection of patterns, books, and fabrics.

Little Quilt Company's Facebook page has posts about new patterns, books, and fabrics and an occasional peek at Kim's latest work.

Other Kim Schaefer titles (also available as eBooks, unless noted otherwise):

No eBook available

Available as eBook only

Great Titles and Products

from C&T PUBLISHING *and* stashBOOKS.

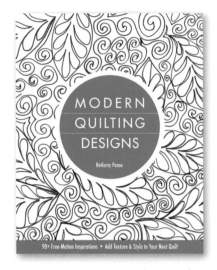

MODERN QUILTING DESIGNS

Bethany Pease

90+ Free-Motion Inspirations • Add Texture & Style to Your Next Quilt

Ultimate 3-in-1
COLOR
TOOL
Updated 3rd Edition

816 Colors with CMYK, RGB & HEX Formulas!

24 Color Cards with Numbered Swatches

5 Color Plans for Each Color

2 Value Finders Red & Green

Joen Wolfrom

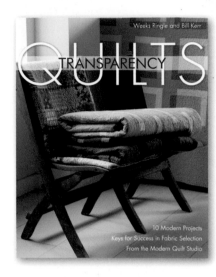

Weeks Ringle and Bill Kerr

TRANSPARENCY QUILTS

10 Modern Projects
Keys for Success in Fabric Selection
From the Modern Quilt Studio

Charlotte Warr Andersen

Bonus! Free Leather Ruler Tape

One Line at a Time, Encore

35 NEW GEOMETRIC MACHINE-QUILTING DESIGNS

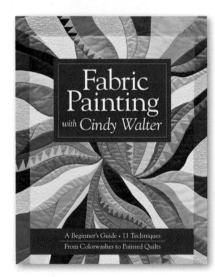

Fabric Painting with Cindy Walter

A Beginner's Guide • 11 Techniques
From Colorwashes to Painted Quilts

SCRAP REPUBLIC

8 QUILT PROJECTS FOR THOSE WHO LOVE COLOR

Emily Cier

Available at your local retailer or **www.ctpub.com** *or* **800-284-1114**

For a list of other fine books from C&T Publishing, visit our website to view our catalog online.

C&T PUBLISHING, INC.
P.O. Box 1456
Lafayette, CA 94549
800-284-1114

Email: ctinfo@ctpub.com
Website: www.ctpub.com

C&T Publishing's professional photography services are now available to the public. Visit us at www.ctmediaservices.com.

Tips and Techniques *can be found at www.ctpub.com > Consumer Resources > Quiltmaking Basics: Tips & Techniques for Quiltmaking & More*

For quilting supplies:

COTTON PATCH
1025 Brown Ave.
Lafayette, CA 94549
Store: 925-284-1177
Mail order: 925-283-7883

Email: CottonPa@aol.com
Website: www.quiltusa.com

Note: Fabrics shown may not be currently available, as fabric manufacturers keep most fabrics in print for only a short time.